**Master NLP with Hugging Face: A Fine-tuning**

**Toolkit**

# Contents

# Chapter 1: Demystifying Natural Language Processing (NLP) and Transformers

- **Unlocking the Power of Language:** Our journey begins with defining NLP. Imagine a world where computers can grasp the nuances of human language – the sarcasm in a friend's text, the hidden emotions in a customer review, or the intricate details in a scientific paper. NLP strives to bridge this gap, enabling computers to process and analyze human language in a meaningful way.

- **A Range of NLP Tasks:** NLP isn't a one-trick pony! It encompasses a vast array of applications that impact our daily lives. We'll explore tasks like:

  - **Text Classification:** Imagine a spam filter that intelligently separates important emails from unwanted advertisements. This is text classification in action! It allows computers to categorize text data based on predefined criteria.

- **Sentiment Analysis:** Ever wondered how companies understand customer satisfaction through online reviews? Sentiment analysis plays a crucial role here. It helps computers decipher the emotional tone of text, whether it's positive, negative, or neutral.

- **Machine Translation:** Have you ever used a translation app to bridge the language gap? Machine translation is a core NLP task that allows computers to translate text from one language to another, breaking down communication barriers.

- **Question Answering:** Imagine a system that can answer your questions directly from a vast amount of written text. This is the power of question answering, where computers can retrieve relevant information based on your query.

- **And there's more!** NLP extends beyond these core tasks, with applications in areas like text summarization, speech recognition, and even creative writing!

- **The NLP Challenge: Cracking the Code of Language:** Human language is beautiful yet complex. Understanding sarcasm, deciphering double meanings, and adapting to context are all challenges NLP grapples with. We'll delve into these complexities to understand why NLP requires sophisticated techniques.

- **Traditional NLP Techniques: Paving the Way:** Before the rise of Deep Learning, NLP relied on approaches like rule-based systems, where programmers defined a set of rules for computers to follow. We'll also explore statistical methods that analyzed large amounts of text data to identify patterns and relationships.

- **The Deep Learning Revolution:** The emergence of Deep Learning, a powerful branch of Artificial Intelligence, has revolutionized NLP. Deep learning algorithms, particularly neural networks, can learn complex patterns from data without the need for explicit rules. This has led to significant advancements in NLP capabilities.

- **Introducing Transformers: The NLP Game Changers:** Amongst Deep Learning architectures, Transformers have emerged as the dominant force in NLP. These specialized neural networks excel at capturing long-range dependencies within language, allowing them to understand the relationships between words even when they are far apart in a sentence. This is a significant advantage over traditional methods.

- **Transformers vs. Traditional Methods: Why the Shift?** Traditional NLP techniques often struggled to capture the intricate relationships within language. Transformers, with their ability to analyze the context of a word based on its entire sentence, can overcome these limitations. We'll explore specific examples of how Transformers address these challenges and showcase their superior performance in NLP tasks.

**Chapter 2: Unveiling Hugging Face Transformers and the Hub**

Get ready to meet Hugging Face, a key player in the NLP revolution:

- **Hugging Face: The Hub of the NLP Community:** Hugging Face is more than just a platform; it's a vibrant community of NLP enthusiasts, researchers, and developers. They foster collaboration by providing open-source tools and resources, making NLP advancements accessible to everyone.

- **The Hugging Face Transformers Library: Your NLP Toolkit:** Buckle up for an introduction to the Hugging Face Transformers library, a user-friendly Python library that simplifies working with Transformer models. This library provides pre-built code structures and functionalities, allowing you to focus on your specific NLP task without getting bogged down in the underlying complexities.

- **Why Use Hugging Face Transformers?** Here's why the Hugging Face Transformers library is a game-changer:

- **Ease of Use:** Forget about writing complex code from scratch. The library offers a user-friendly interface that makes it easy to use pre-trained models for various NLP tasks.

- **Pre-trained Models Galore:** Imagine having access to a vast collection of pre-trained Transformer models, fine-tuned for specific tasks. The Hugging Face Model Hub provides exactly that, saving you the time and resources required to train your own models from scratch.

# Part 2: Getting Started with Hugging Face

# Transformers

Welcome to the exciting world of hands-on NLP with Hugging Face Transformers! In this part, we'll equip you with the practical skills to set up your environment, explore the treasure trove of pre-trained models, and finally, leverage them for real-world NLP tasks.

## Chapter 3: Installation and Setup - Building Your NLP Toolkit

Before we embark on our NLP adventures, let's ensure you have the necessary tools. This chapter will be your guide to setting up your development environment:

- **Python and Essential Libraries:** We'll start by installing the foundation – Python, the versatile programming language commonly used in NLP. We'll also introduce you to essential libraries like NumPy, a workhorse for numerical computations, and PyTorch (or TensorFlow), powerful deep learning frameworks that provide the computational muscle for your NLP projects.

## Installing Hugging Face Transformers: Unleashing the NLP Powerhouse

The moment we've all been waiting for! Here's where we welcome the star of the show – the Hugging Face

Transformers library. This library is the powerhouse that grants you access to a vast arsenal of pre-trained Transformers, ready to tackle your NLP challenges. We'll guide you through a smooth installation process using pip, the go-to package manager for Python.

**Why pip?**

pip is an incredibly convenient and widely used tool for installing Python packages like Hugging Face Transformers. It simplifies the process by handling dependencies – other libraries the Transformers library relies on to function properly. With pip, you won't have to download and install each dependency manually, saving you time and effort.

**The Installation Process:**

1. **Open your Terminal or Command Prompt:** This is where you'll interact with your computer using text commands. For Windows users, you can search for "Command Prompt" or "PowerShell." Mac and Linux users can typically access the terminal by pressing command + space and searching for "Terminal."

2. **Activate your Virtual Environment (Optional but Recommended):** Virtual environments are highly recommended for Python development. They isolate project dependencies, preventing conflicts with other Python projects on your system. If you're unfamiliar with virtual environments, no worries! This book will

provide a brief introduction to their benefits and how to create one.

3. **Install Hugging Face Transformers:** Once you're in your terminal or command prompt (and optionally within your virtual environment), type the following command and press Enter:

Bash

```
pip install transformers
```

pip will take care of downloading and installing the Hugging Face Transformers library along with all its necessary dependencies. The installation process might take a few minutes depending on your internet speed.

4. **Verification:** Once the installation is complete, you can verify if everything is working as

expected. Type the following command in your terminal and press Enter:

Python

```
python -c "from transformers import pipeline;
print(pipeline('sentiment-analysis')('I hate you'))"
```

This code snippet attempts to use a pre-trained sentiment analysis model from the Transformers library. If the installation was successful, you should see an output indicating the sentiment of the provided sentence, for example:

```
[{'label': 'NEGATIVE', 'score': 0.9991129040718079}]
```

Congratulations! You've successfully installed the Hugging Face Transformers library and are now ready to explore the vast potential of pre-trained Transformers for your NLP projects.

- **Verifying Your Setup with a Test Drive:** Once everything is installed, we'll show you how to run a simple test script included in the Hugging Face Transformers library. This ensures your environment is configured correctly and ready to tackle NLP tasks with Transformers.

## Advanced Model Fine-Tuning with Transformers

In recent years, transformers have become the backbone of many state-of-the-art NLP models, thanks to their ability to capture long-range dependencies in textual data through self-attention mechanisms. Hugging Face's Transformers library provides an easy-to-use interface to access these powerful models, but fine-tuning them for specific tasks requires an understanding of the inner workings of these models and the best practices for optimizing their performance on specialized datasets.

Fine-tuning a pre-trained transformer model involves taking a model that has already been trained on a large general corpus of text, such as books or web pages, and adapting it to a specific task or domain by continuing its training on a task-specific dataset. This process is crucial for NLP tasks such as text classification, sentiment analysis, named entity recognition, and more, as it enables the model to specialize its knowledge and improve its performance in a narrower context.

At the heart of transformers is the self-attention mechanism, which allows models to focus on different parts of an input sequence when making predictions. This is particularly useful for tasks involving complex linguistic structures, such as understanding long sentences or extracting meaning from ambiguous phrases. However, fine-tuning these models for particular tasks requires more than just loading a pre-trained model and running it on your data. To truly maximize performance, you must carefully manage the training process, adjust hyperparameters, and address challenges like overfitting or data imbalance.

The first step in fine-tuning is choosing the right pre-trained model. Hugging Face offers a variety of models, from the original BERT model for masked language modeling to GPT-3 for generative tasks and T5 for text-to-text transformations. Each of these models comes with different strengths, depending on the task. For instance, BERT is highly effective for tasks like question answering and sentence classification, while GPT-3 excels in generating coherent text based on prompts.

Once a model is chosen, the next step is preparing the dataset. Hugging Face provides several utilities for processing text data, including tokenization, padding, and truncation, to ensure that the model can efficiently process your input text. Tokenization breaks down text into smaller units, such as words or subwords, that the model can understand. The library also supports multiple tokenization strategies, from Byte-Pair Encoding (BPE) to WordPiece, depending on the model being used.

After tokenization, it's essential to create the correct input format for training. This often involves aligning the tokenized text with the model's expected input structure, such as adding attention masks or specifying which tokens are part of the input and which are part of the labels. Hugging Face provides utilities that automatically handle this, but for more advanced use cases, manual adjustments might be necessary.

Training a transformer model involves selecting the appropriate loss function and optimization strategy. For tasks like classification, the standard approach is to use cross-entropy loss, while for regression tasks, a mean squared error loss might be more appropriate. Optimization is typically performed using gradient descent-based methods, with the Adam optimizer being the most commonly used for transformer models. However, fine-tuning requires careful management of learning rates to avoid overfitting and to achieve stable training.

One advanced technique is to use learning rate schedules, such as the warm-up and decay schedules commonly used in transformer training. These schedules adjust the learning rate during training, initially starting with a smaller rate and gradually increasing it before decaying it toward the end of the training process. This helps the model converge more efficiently, especially when fine-tuning on smaller datasets.

Overfitting is a common challenge when fine-tuning large models on task-specific datasets, particularly when the dataset is small. One way to mitigate overfitting is through regularization techniques such as dropout, where a portion of the network's connections are randomly turned off during training, forcing the model to learn more robust representations. Additionally, early stopping can be used to halt training once the model's performance on a validation set starts to degrade, thus preventing overtraining.

Data augmentation is another advanced technique that can help improve model performance, particularly in situations where the dataset is limited. By generating synthetic examples through techniques such as back-translation or paraphrasing, you can expose the model to a broader range of variations of the data. Hugging Face's datasets library includes numerous pre-processed datasets that can be augmented for use in training, making it easier to apply these techniques.

Fine-tuning also involves hyperparameter tuning to ensure the best possible performance. While Hugging Face offers default settings for many models, manually adjusting the learning rate, batch size, and number of training epochs can significantly impact the model's final performance. Hyperparameter optimization techniques, such as grid search, random search, and Bayesian optimization, can be used to systematically explore different combinations of hyperparameters to find the most effective configuration for your task.

Another important consideration when fine-tuning transformer models is handling imbalanced datasets. In many real-world tasks, certain classes or categories are underrepresented, leading to biased models. Techniques such as class weighting, oversampling the minority class, and undersampling the majority class can help address this imbalance. Additionally, adversarial training methods can be applied to make the model more robust to perturbations in the data, improving its generalization ability.

One of the significant advantages of Hugging Face's ecosystem is the ease of integrating various tools into the fine-tuning workflow. For instance, the Trainer class simplifies many aspects of training and evaluation, such as logging, checkpointing, and gradient accumulation, all of which are crucial when dealing with large datasets and long training times. The transformers library also integrates with popular deep learning frameworks like TensorFlow and PyTorch, allowing you to leverage the strengths of both ecosystems.

Finally, evaluating a fine-tuned model involves using a set of appropriate metrics for your task, such as accuracy, precision, recall, F1 score, or BLEU score for translation tasks. Hugging Face provides built-in evaluation metrics, but for more specialized tasks, you may need to define custom metrics. Additionally, model interpretability can be enhanced using tools like SHAP or LIME to understand which parts of the input were most influential in the model's decision-making process.

With these advanced fine-tuning techniques, you can push the boundaries of what's possible with transformer-based models, leveraging the full potential of Hugging Face's libraries to achieve state-of-the-art performance in a wide range of NLP tasks. Fine-tuning is a critical step in adapting large pre-trained models to your specific needs, and mastering these techniques will allow you to build robust, efficient, and highly specialized NLP applications.

## Optimizing Transformer Performance for Specialized Tasks

While the basic process of fine-tuning involves adjusting a model's weights to optimize performance on a specific task, advanced optimization techniques allow for further refinement and significant improvements. In this chapter, we delve deeper into some of the most effective strategies for fine-tuning transformer models, focusing on optimizations that go beyond standard approaches.

Transformers, particularly large ones like GPT-3 and T5, are known for their impressive performance across a wide range of NLP tasks. However, they are also resource-intensive, requiring substantial computational power for training and fine-tuning. One of the most important aspects of optimizing transformer models is managing the trade-off between model performance and computational efficiency. With the increasing size of transformer models, training and fine-tuning can become prohibitively expensive. As such, it is crucial to explore optimization strategies that reduce resource consumption without sacrificing accuracy.

Model pruning is one such technique. By selectively removing certain weights or neurons from a trained model, you can reduce its size and make it more efficient, all while maintaining much of its original performance. Pruning can be done by targeting low-importance weights—those that contribute little to the model's predictions—and removing them. Hugging Face's library offers tools to apply pruning techniques to transformer models, allowing you to reduce model complexity and memory footprint.

Another advanced optimization technique is knowledge distillation, where a smaller model (the student) is trained to mimic the behavior of a larger model (the teacher). This technique is particularly useful for deploying transformer models on devices with limited resources, such as mobile phones or edge devices. The student model learns to approximate the teacher's output, allowing it to achieve similar levels of performance while requiring fewer parameters.

Furthermore, reducing the model's precision through techniques like quantization can improve performance without compromising too much accuracy. Quantization involves converting floating-point model weights into lower precision, such as int8, which reduces memory requirements and accelerates inference. Hugging Face provides tools to convert models to lower precision and to run them on hardware that supports quantized models.

Distributed training is another important aspect of optimizing performance for large transformer models. Fine-tuning a massive model like GPT-3 on a single machine can be time-consuming and computationally expensive. Distributed training splits the workload across multiple machines, allowing you to fine-tune models faster and more efficiently. Hugging Face's integration with popular distributed training frameworks like PyTorch Lightning and DeepSpeed makes it easier to scale training across multiple GPUs or even multiple nodes.

One aspect of transformer performance that is often overlooked is the optimization of the tokenization process. Tokenization is a crucial step in transforming raw text into input that a model can process. Optimizing tokenization not only speeds up preprocessing but also improves the model's efficiency by minimizing the size of the input sequences. Hugging Face provides tools to experiment with different tokenization techniques, such as subword-based tokenizers like Byte-Pair Encoding (BPE) and SentencePiece.

In addition to these techniques, an advanced aspect of fine-tuning transformers involves customizing the training process itself. For example, gradient accumulation allows you to accumulate gradients over several mini-batches before performing a weight update, which can help stabilize training when dealing with large datasets or when memory is limited. Similarly, mixed precision training, where operations are carried out using both 16-bit and 32-bit floating-point numbers, can significantly speed up training times and reduce memory usage.

Evaluating the performance of fine-tuned transformer models is crucial to ensure that the optimizations have been successful. Metrics such as accuracy, BLEU score, and perplexity are commonly used for various NLP tasks. However, in advanced applications, you might also need to consider domain-specific evaluation metrics or metrics that reflect the model's efficiency, such as inference time and memory usage. Tools like Hugging Face's datasets and evaluate libraries allow you to easily compute these metrics during the fine-tuning process and adjust hyperparameters accordingly.

# Leveraging Transfer Learning for Domain-Specific NLP Tasks

Transfer learning is a powerful strategy that allows models to leverage pre-existing knowledge learned from one domain and apply it to another, typically more specialized task. This approach is especially valuable in the field of NLP, where training deep models from scratch requires vast amounts of labeled data and computational resources. Hugging Face's Transformers library provides an excellent framework for applying transfer learning, making it accessible even for smaller organizations or individuals with limited resources.

At its core, transfer learning in NLP involves starting with a model pre-trained on a massive general corpus of text, such as the English Wikipedia or a large collection of news articles. These models have learned a variety of language patterns, grammatical structures, and semantic relationships, which can then be fine-tuned to perform specific tasks, such as medical document classification or sentiment analysis of financial reports.

The key advantage of transfer learning lies in the ability to adapt pre-trained models to new domains with relatively small amounts of task-specific data. For example, fine-tuning a model like BERT on a legal dataset allows the model to learn the specific terminology and structures common in legal texts, thus improving its performance on tasks such as contract review, legal document summarization, or case law classification. The process of fine-tuning involves updating only a small portion of the model's parameters, allowing it to specialize without needing to relearn everything from scratch.

One common challenge in domain-specific transfer learning is the potential mismatch between the general pre-trained corpus and the target domain. For example, a model pre-trained on news articles may not perform as well on medical data, which contains highly specialized vocabulary. To overcome this, many practitioners opt to first pre-train a model on a domain-specific corpus before fine-tuning it on task-specific data. For instance, models like BioBERT and ClinicalBERT have been pre-trained on large medical and clinical corpora, allowing them to capture domain-specific language before fine-tuning on tasks such as disease classification or medical question answering.

In addition to domain adaptation, transfer learning can be used for more specialized tasks that require deep semantic understanding. For example, in the field of dialogue systems, fine-tuning a transformer model like GPT-3 or T5 can allow it to generate highly context-aware responses for customer support, virtual assistants, or social media chatbots. By leveraging the knowledge already encoded in the pre-trained model, transfer learning accelerates the process of achieving high performance in a target application.

Another key consideration when applying transfer learning is the method of fine-tuning. Standard fine-tuning typically involves updating the model's weights based on task-specific data. However, advanced techniques like multi-task learning or few-shot learning can be incorporated to further boost performance. Multi-task learning allows a model to be trained on several tasks simultaneously, encouraging the model to learn more generalized features that are beneficial across multiple domains. Few-shot learning, on the other hand, aims to enable models to learn from only a handful of examples, making it particularly useful in cases where labeled data is scarce.

When implementing transfer learning, practitioners must also carefully monitor the model's performance during fine-tuning to avoid overfitting, especially when dealing with limited data. Regularization techniques like dropout and weight decay can be applied to mitigate overfitting, while strategies like data augmentation and synthetic data generation can help generate additional training examples. Additionally, techniques such as early stopping and cross-validation are critical to ensure that the model generalizes well to unseen data.

Overall, transfer learning has become a cornerstone of modern NLP, enabling the efficient development of high-performance models for specialized tasks. By leveraging pre-trained models and domain-specific datasets, it is possible to achieve state-of-the-art performance with less data and computational resources than traditional training methods would require.

## Advanced Techniques for Model Interpretability and Debugging

As transformer-based models become increasingly sophisticated, understanding how they make decisions has become a critical area of research and application. Interpretability and debugging are particularly important when these models are deployed in real-world applications, where their decisions can have significant consequences. Hugging Face provides several tools and methodologies to help practitioners not only build high-performing models but also make them interpretable and understandable.

The first step in model interpretability is understanding which parts of the input text the model is attending to when making predictions. Since transformer models rely on attention mechanisms, they process input data by assigning different attention weights to different tokens. These attention weights determine how much focus the model places on each token when making predictions. By visualizing these attention weights, practitioners can gain insights into the model's decision-making process.

Hugging Face provides built-in functions to visualize attention maps for models like BERT and GPT. These attention maps show which words or subwords the model focuses on at each layer of the network, allowing users to see how the model interprets the input. For example, in a sentence like "The bank is next to the river," an attention map might reveal that the model focuses on the word "bank" when predicting its meaning in the context of finance, versus focusing on the word "river" when predicting it as a geographical feature. These visualizations can help identify potential biases or errors in how the model processes information.

In addition to attention maps, techniques like Layer-wise Relevance Propagation (LRP) and SHAP (Shapley Additive Explanations) can provide more granular insights into model predictions. LRP works by decomposing the output of a model into contributions from each input token, helping to identify which parts of the input are most influential in the final prediction. SHAP, on the other hand, provides a unified framework for explaining model outputs by quantifying the contribution of each feature to the final decision. Hugging Face's integration with these libraries makes it easy to implement and visualize these interpretability techniques.

Another important aspect of model interpretability is identifying and mitigating biases that may be present in the model. Transformer models, especially those trained on large text corpora scraped from the web, are prone to inheriting and amplifying the biases present in the data. These biases can manifest in various ways, such as gender, racial, or ethnic biases, which may lead to discriminatory or unfair predictions. Tools like the AI Fairness 360 toolkit from IBM and the Fairness Indicators library from TensorFlow can be integrated into Hugging Face models to detect and mitigate such biases.

Beyond interpretability, debugging is an essential skill in fine-tuning transformer models. Debugging involves understanding why a model is making incorrect predictions and identifying potential issues in the data, model architecture, or training process. One of the most common challenges in fine-tuning transformer models is the problem of catastrophic forgetting, where a model forgets previously learned knowledge when fine-tuned on a new task. This is especially problematic when working with small or noisy datasets.

To mitigate catastrophic forgetting, several techniques can be applied. One such technique is elastic weight consolidation (EWC), which helps prevent the model from forgetting important parameters by applying a penalty to changes in weights that are crucial to the model's performance on previous tasks. Another technique is incremental learning, where the model is gradually fine-tuned on new tasks while retaining its ability to perform well on older tasks.

Another debugging challenge is overfitting, which occurs when a model performs well on training data but fails to generalize to unseen examples. Regularization techniques, such as dropout and weight decay, are commonly used to address overfitting, but careful monitoring of the training and validation loss curves is also necessary. If the model's performance on the validation set starts to degrade while its performance on the training set continues to improve, early stopping can be applied to halt the training process and prevent further overfitting.

Finally, debugging also involves understanding how the model interacts with external factors, such as external libraries, hardware, and infrastructure. For example, if a model's inference time is slower than expected, it may be due to inefficient tokenization or issues with batch processing. Profiling tools, such as PyTorch's built-in profiler, can help identify bottlenecks in the model's pipeline, allowing for optimization of data loading, GPU usage, and model inference.

Incorporating interpretability and debugging into the fine-tuning workflow is crucial for developing trustworthy and reliable transformer-based models. By gaining a deeper understanding of how models make decisions and addressing common issues like

bias and overfitting, practitioners can build more

transparent, fair, and robust NLP systems.

## Scaling Up Transformer Models for Production-Grade Systems

Deploying transformer-based models in production

systems requires careful consideration of several

factors, including scalability, latency, and resource utilization. As models grow in size and complexity, they require more computational power, memory, and storage. Hugging Face's ecosystem provides several tools to help scale up models for real-world applications, ensuring they can handle large volumes of data and provide fast responses.

One of the key challenges in scaling transformer models is managing their memory footprint. Large models, like GPT-3 and T5, have hundreds of billions of parameters, making them difficult to run on standard hardware. To address this challenge, model compression techniques such as quantization and distillation can be applied. Quantization reduces the precision of model weights, converting them from 32-bit floating-point values to lower precision, such as 16-bit or 8-bit integers. This can reduce memory usage and increase inference speed without significantly compromising model performance.

Knowledge distillation is another technique used to scale up models. In this approach, a smaller model (the student) is trained to mimic the predictions of a larger model (the teacher). This allows the smaller model to approximate the performance of the larger model while requiring fewer resources. Hugging Face's transformers library supports distillation, making it easier to deploy smaller models with high efficiency.

Another key consideration in scaling transformer models is distributed training. Fine-tuning large models on a single machine can be time-consuming and resource-intensive, especially when working with limited hardware. Distributed training, where the model is split across multiple devices or machines, can significantly speed up the training process. Hugging Face offers integrations with distributed training frameworks like DeepSpeed and Hugging Face Accelerate, enabling practitioners to scale training to multiple GPUs or even across multiple nodes in a data center.

To optimize inference speed, it's also important to consider the deployment environment. For real-time applications, such as chatbots or voice assistants, low-latency inference is critical. Techniques like batching, model pruning, and offloading some computations to specialized hardware (e.g., TPUs or custom accelerators) can help reduce inference time and improve response times. Hugging Face's optimum library provides tools for optimizing models for different deployment environments, making it easier to deploy models on edge devices, mobile platforms, or cloud-based systems.

When deploying transformer models at scale, practitioners must also consider monitoring and maintaining the models in production. Continuous monitoring helps identify performance degradation, data drift, and other issues that may arise over time. Hugging Face's datasets library can be used to continuously monitor the model's input and output, flagging any discrepancies or unexpected behavior. In addition, logging tools like TensorBoard can be integrated to track model performance metrics and visualize the model's behavior over time.

Scaling transformer models for production systems is a complex but rewarding task. By employing strategies like model compression, distributed training, and inference optimization, practitioners can deploy large models at scale while maintaining high performance and low latency.

**Integrating Multimodal Transformers for Complex Tasks**

While traditional transformer models like BERT and GPT are primarily designed for text-based tasks, recent advancements in multimodal transformers have expanded their capabilities to handle multiple types of data, including images, audio, and video. This integration allows these models to perform complex tasks that involve a combination of modalities, such as visual question answering, image captioning, and audio-based speech recognition.

Multimodal transformers work by combining different types of inputs—such as text and images—into a unified representation. These models learn to process and align information from each modality and use this combined representation to perform tasks that require an understanding of both the visual and textual elements. Hugging Face provides several pre-trained multimodal models, such as VisualBERT and CLIP (Contrastive Language-Image Pretraining), that can be fine-tuned for specific tasks.

The challenge with multimodal transformers lies in effectively processing and aligning data from different modalities. For example, when working with both text and images, the model needs to learn how to relate visual features, such as objects and scenes, with corresponding textual descriptions. One common approach is to use cross-attention mechanisms, which allow the model to learn interactions between modalities. For instance, a multimodal model could attend to specific parts of an image while generating a caption that describes that part, effectively bridging the gap between the visual and textual representations.

One application of multimodal transformers is in the field of video understanding, where the model must process both the visual content of a video and any accompanying speech or subtitles. Models like VideoBERT and UniVL (Unified Vision-Language Transformer) are designed to handle this type of input, enabling tasks like video captioning and temporal question answering. These models are trained to understand the temporal relationships between frames in a video and the corresponding textual or spoken content.

Another area where multimodal transformers are making an impact is in healthcare, where they are being used to analyze medical imaging data alongside patient records or clinical notes. By combining visual and textual data, multimodal models can assist in tasks like medical image diagnosis, where they can help identify anomalies in X-rays or MRIs while also considering relevant textual information from patient reports.

The integration of multimodal transformers opens up new possibilities for NLP applications, enabling models to handle more complex and richer data types. However, fine-tuning these models requires careful handling of each modality's unique characteristics. Text data, for example, requires tokenization and embedding techniques, while images need to be processed using convolutional neural networks (CNNs) to extract features. Hugging Face's transformers library, in collaboration with other frameworks like PyTorch and TensorFlow, provides the necessary tools to seamlessly integrate these modalities into a unified pipeline.

As multimodal models continue to evolve, their potential to solve complex, real-world problems will only increase. For now, practitioners can take advantage of the pre-trained models and fine-tuning tools provided by Hugging Face to explore the possibilities of multimodal NLP applications.

## Scaling Transformer Models for Real-Time Applications

Scaling transformer models to handle real-time applications, such as chatbots, recommendation systems, and customer support tools, is essential for delivering high-performance and low-latency responses. One of the main challenges with large models is the computational cost associated with running inference in real time. In this chapter, we will explore several strategies for scaling transformer models to ensure they can operate efficiently in production environments.

Optimizing for Inference Speed

Inference speed is crucial when deploying large models in real-time systems. Large models tend to be slow due to their extensive parameter count and complex computations. Here are several techniques to improve inference speed:

- **Model Pruning**: Removing less important weights from the model can reduce its size and improve inference speed without compromising too much on accuracy. This technique is particularly useful when dealing with large transformer models, which often have redundancies.

- **Quantization**: Quantization involves reducing the precision of the weights and activations, typically from floating-point precision to lower bit-width (e.g., 8-bit integers). This can drastically reduce the model size and speed up computations while maintaining an acceptable level of performance.

- **Knowledge Distillation**: This technique involves training a smaller, more efficient model (the "student") to mimic the behavior of a larger model (the "teacher"). The student model, once trained, can provide similar outputs while being much faster and more resource-efficient.

- **Batching and Parallelism**: In scenarios where multiple requests need to be handled simultaneously, batching requests together can improve throughput. Additionally, parallel processing across multiple GPUs or distributed systems can help scale the inference workload.

For real-time applications, maintaining low latency is just as important as having a high throughput. By employing techniques such as model pruning, quantization, and knowledge distillation, organizations can reduce the computational burden and speed up inference times. Hugging Face's integration with hardware accelerators such as TPUs and GPUs also enables developers to implement these optimizations effectively.

Cloud Deployment Considerations

When deploying transformer models in production, especially for real-time applications, it's important to consider cloud infrastructure options. Using cloud services like AWS, Azure, or Google Cloud can help provide scalability and flexibility. These services often include hardware accelerators such as TPUs and GPUs, which can be used to speed up both training and inference.

However, cloud deployment also introduces challenges, such as latency due to data transfer between the model and the user. To mitigate this, some applications benefit from edge computing, where models are deployed closer to the end user to reduce the round-trip time. Hugging Face's optimum library is designed to support edge devices, making it easier to deploy models in environments with limited resources.

Optimizing transformer models for real-time applications requires a multifaceted approach. Techniques such as pruning, quantization, and distributed processing are essential for scaling models efficiently. Additionally, leveraging cloud infrastructure and edge computing can help maintain low-latency responses, ensuring high-quality user experiences.

## Leveraging Transfer Learning and Fine-Tuning with Hugging Face

Transfer learning has become a central technique in NLP due to its ability to use pre-trained models and adapt them for specific tasks with relatively small amounts of additional training. This approach not only saves time and resources but also significantly improves model performance, especially when training data for a specific task is limited.

The power of transfer learning lies in the fact that models like BERT, GPT-3, and T5 have been pre-trained on massive corpora, enabling them to capture broad language knowledge. These models can then be fine-tuned on task-specific datasets, allowing them to specialize in specific domains or tasks such as sentiment analysis, named entity recognition, or machine translation.

## Fine-tuning Pre-trained Models

Fine-tuning a pre-trained model with Hugging Face's transformers library is an efficient and effective way to adapt the model for a particular task. The general process involves selecting a pre-trained model, loading it with Hugging Face's API, and then fine-tuning it on the target dataset. During this fine-tuning process, the model's weights are updated to make it more suitable for the specific task while retaining the knowledge it gained during pre-training.

Hugging Face offers an extensive collection of pre-trained models that are available for fine-tuning across a wide range of NLP tasks. These models, including BERT, RoBERTa, and GPT, are ready to be fine-tuned on your custom data, enabling rapid prototyping and development. For example, fine-tuning a BERT model for sentiment analysis may only require training for a few epochs on a small dataset of labeled text.

Transfer learning can also be used for multi-task learning, where a single model is fine-tuned for multiple tasks simultaneously. This approach is particularly useful when the tasks share similarities, as the model can leverage shared knowledge to improve performance across all tasks.

Optimizing the Fine-Tuning Process

Fine-tuning a model effectively requires careful consideration of various hyperparameters, such as learning rate, batch size, and the number of epochs. Hugging Face's Trainer class simplifies this process by automating much of the training pipeline, including optimization, evaluation, and logging. You can also customize the training process by using callbacks and integration with third-party libraries like Weights & Biases for more advanced monitoring.

Hyperparameter optimization is a key aspect of fine-tuning. Using techniques like grid search, random search, or Bayesian optimization, practitioners can identify the optimal combination of hyperparameters for their task. Hugging Face's optuna integration can be used to automate this process, making it easier to find the best configuration for fine-tuning a model.

Transfer learning and fine-tuning provide a powerful way to adapt large pre-trained models to specific tasks with minimal effort. By leveraging Hugging Face's tools and libraries, developers can save significant time and resources while achieving state-of-the-art results across a variety of NLP applications.

# Building Robust Models with Active Learning

Active learning is a machine learning paradigm that allows models to improve their performance by actively selecting the most informative samples from a dataset. Instead of relying on a large labeled dataset, active learning enables a model to iteratively query an oracle (often a human annotator) to label specific data points that are most likely to improve the model's performance. This is particularly useful in situations where labeling data is expensive or time-consuming.

In the context of natural language processing, active learning can be used to enhance the performance of transformer models on tasks such as sentiment analysis, question answering, and named entity recognition. By strategically selecting the most informative samples, active learning reduces the amount of labeled data required to achieve high accuracy, making it an attractive option for domains with limited labeled data.

## The Active Learning Process

The active learning process typically follows an iterative cycle. First, a model is trained on a small set of labeled data. Once trained, the model is used to predict labels for a larger pool of unlabeled data. The model then identifies the most uncertain or ambiguous samples, which are sent to an oracle (human annotator) for labeling. The labeled data is added to the training set, and the model is retrained.

This process continues until the model reaches an

acceptable level of performance.

In practice, there are several strategies for selecting

uncertain samples. One common approach is

uncertainty sampling, where the model selects

examples for which it is least confident in its

predictions. Another strategy is query-by-committee,

where multiple models are trained, and the examples

on which they disagree the most are selected for

labeling.

Hugging Face's transformers library can be used in

conjunction with active learning techniques to fine-

tune models more efficiently. Once a model is fine-tuned on a small set of labeled data, the model can be used to identify uncertain samples from a larger corpus. These samples can then be manually labeled and added to the training set to improve the model's performance.

Active learning is particularly beneficial when dealing with domain-specific tasks, where acquiring labeled data may be expensive or challenging. For example, in legal or medical domains, the cost of manually labeling data can be prohibitive. Active learning helps optimize the labeling process by focusing on the data that will provide the most value to the model.

Challenges and Considerations

While active learning can significantly reduce the

amount of labeled data needed, it does come with challenges. One potential issue is the risk of overfitting to a limited set of labeled examples, which can result in poor generalization. To mitigate this, it is essential to ensure diversity in the samples selected for labeling. Additionally, the quality of the labeled data must be maintained to prevent introducing noise into the training process.

Active learning is a powerful technique for building robust models with limited labeled data. By using active learning, developers can improve model performance and reduce the costs associated with manual labeling, making it an essential tool for real-world NLP applications. Hugging Face provides the tools necessary to integrate active learning with transformer models, enabling efficient model training even in resource-constrained environments.

**Chapter 4: Exploring the Hugging Face Model Hub - A Marketplace for NLP Solutions**

The Hugging Face Model Hub is a game-changer for NLP enthusiasts! This chapter equips you with the skills to navigate this vast repository effectively, allowing you to find pre-trained models that fit your specific needs:

- **A Wealth of Pre-trained Models:** We'll delve into the different types of models available on the Hub. Discover models pre-trained for various NLP tasks like text classification (spam filtering!), sentiment analysis (deciphering emotions in text), question answering (think chatbots!), machine translation (breaking down language barriers), and even text summarization (condensing lengthy documents).

- **Search Like a Pro:** Imagine needing a model for sentiment analysis of social media posts. We'll guide you through the Hub's advanced search functionalities, allowing you to filter models based on specific criteria. You can search by task (sentiment analysis), language (English, Spanish, etc.), and even model architecture (different types of Transformers with varying strengths).

- **Model Cards: Decoding the Details:** Each model on the Hub comes with a detailed "model card." This chapter will explain how to interpret these cards, which provide valuable information about the model's performance on benchmark datasets, the type of data it was trained on, and any usage guidelines or limitations to consider.

- **Downloading and Saving Models for Offline Use:** Once you've identified the perfect model for your project, we'll show you how to download it for offline use. This allows you to leverage the model's power even without an internet connection, making your NLP project more portable and efficient.

## Chapter 5: Loading and Using Pre-trained Models (Text Classification, Question Answering, Summarization, etc.)

Now comes the fun part – putting pre-trained models to work! This chapter will showcase how to use these models for various NLP tasks:

- **Loading Pre-trained Models:** We'll explore the functionalities of the Hugging Face Transformers library that allow you to effortlessly load a pre-trained model from the Hub.

- **Text Classification in Action:** Imagine a system that can automatically categorize emails as spam or important. We'll build a text classification pipeline using a pre-trained model, allowing you to classify new text data based on predefined categories.

- **Unlocking the Power of Question Answering:** Ever wondered how chatbots answer your questions? We'll demonstrate how to use a pre-trained model for question answering, enabling you to build systems that can retrieve relevant information from text based on user queries.

- **Summarization Made Easy:** Feeling overwhelmed by lengthy documents? We'll introduce you to pre-trained summarization models that can automatically generate concise summaries of text data.

- **Beyond the Basics:** This chapter will provide a glimpse into using pre-trained models for other NLP tasks like sentiment analysis and machine translation. We'll showcase the versatility of the Hugging Face Transformers library and the vast possibilities it unlocks.

By the end of Part 2, you'll be well on your way to

leveraging the power of Hugging Face Transformers

for your NLP projects. You'll be able to navigate the

Model Hub, select appropriate models, and put them

to work on real-world NLP tasks, opening doors to

exciting applications in various domains.

**Part 3: Fine-tuning Hugging Face Models**

## Chapter 6: Understanding Fine-tuning Concepts

This chapter dives deep into the philosophy and practicalities of fine-tuning pre-trained Hugging Face Transformers for your specific NLP tasks.

## The Power of Pre-trained Models

Pre-trained models are the foundation of NLP advancements. These models, trained on massive datasets of text and code, have learned a vast amount of linguistic knowledge. This allows them to perform well on various NLP tasks, from text classification (spam filtering) to sentiment analysis (deciphering emotions in text). Think of them as highly-educated general practitioners in the world of language.

## Limitations of Pre-trained Models

Despite their impressive capabilities, pre-trained models have limitations. Imagine using a model trained on general text for a specific domain like legal documents. The model might struggle to understand the nuances of legal language. Furthermore, pre-trained models can be computationally expensive to train from scratch, requiring significant resources and time.

**The Fine-tuning Philosophy**

Fine-tuning addresses these limitations by leveraging the pre-trained model's existing knowledge and adapting it to your specific task. It's like taking a general doctor and specializing them into a cardiologist by focusing their training on heart-related issues. Here's how it works:

1. **Choose a Pre-trained Model:** Select a pre-trained model from the Hugging Face Model

Hub that aligns with your NLP task (e.g., text classification, sentiment analysis, etc.).

2. **Freeze the Base Layers:** The pre-trained model typically consists of multiple layers, each layer progressively extracting higher-level features from the text. During fine-tuning, we freeze the initial layers (the base) that contain the general linguistic knowledge. These layers have already learned valuable representations of language and don't require significant changes for your specific task.

3. **Fine-tune the Final Layers:** The final layers of the pre-trained model are responsible for the specific task output (e.g., classifying text or generating a sentiment score). These layers are

"unfrozen" and retrained on your labeled data relevant to your specific task. This allows the model to adapt its understanding of language to your domain and data.

**Benefits of Fine-tuning**

Fine-tuning offers several advantages

- **Improved Performance:** By tailoring the model to your specific task and data, you can achieve significantly better results compared to using a generic pre-trained model. Imagine the difference between a general doctor and a cardiologist diagnosing a heart condition.

- **Reduced Training Time:** Since the pre-trained model already has a strong foundation, fine-tuning typically requires less training data and time compared to training a model from scratch. This is because the base layers, containing the general language knowledge, don't need to be re-trained from scratch.

- **Transfer Learning in Action:** Fine-tuning exemplifies transfer learning, a core concept in deep learning. We leverage the knowledge learned from a broader task (pre-trained model) and apply it to a more specific task (your NLP project). Think of it as using your knowledge of general mathematics to excel in a specific area like calculus.

**Challenges of Fine-tuning**

While powerful, fine-tuning comes with its own challenges:

- **Data Requirements:** Fine-tuning requires a sufficient amount of labeled data specific to your task. This data is used to train the final layers of the model. While less data is needed compared to training from scratch, collecting and annotating enough data can be a bottleneck.

- **Overfitting:** There's a risk of the model becoming overly focused on the specific patterns in your training data and performing poorly on unseen data (data it hasn't encountered before). Techniques like data augmentation (artificially creating more training data) and early stopping (stopping training before overfitting occurs) can help mitigate this risk.

# Chapter 7: Data Preparation for Fine-tuning

High-quality data is the fuel for successful fine-tuning! This chapter guides you through the essential steps of preparing your data for fine-tuning pre-trained models.

## Understanding Labeled Data

Fine-tuning relies on labeled data, where each data point (text, sentence, or document) has a corresponding label indicating its category or meaning. For example, in sentiment analysis of movie reviews, each review might be labeled as "positive," "negative," or "neutral." The type of labels required depends on the specific NLP task:

- **Text Classification:** Labels indicate the category each text data point belongs to (e.g., spam or not-spam, positive or negative review).

- **Question Answering:** Labels can be in the form of the answer itself (for extractive QA) or a score indicating how well an answer passage matches the question.

- **Text Summarization:** Labels might be human-written summaries of the documents used for training.

The quality and relevance of your labeled data significantly impact the performance of the fine-tuned model. Strive for data that is:

- **Accurate:** Ensure labels are assigned correctly and consistently. Inconsistencies can confuse the model during training.

- **Representative:** The data should reflect the real-world distribution of the task you're trying to solve. For example, if classifying social media sentiment, ensure your data includes a balanced mix of positive, negative, and neutral posts.

- **Balanced:** If your task involves multiple categories (e.g., sentiment analysis), aim for a balanced distribution of labels across categories.

An imbalanced dataset with very few examples of a specific category can hinder the model's ability to learn that category effectively.

## Data Collection Strategies

There are several ways to collect labeled data for fine-tuning:

- **In-house Data:** If you have access to relevant data within your organization, you can leverage it for labeling. For instance, a company might use its customer support tickets for training a sentiment analysis model.

- **Public Datasets:** Numerous publicly available labeled datasets exist for various NLP tasks. The Hugging Face Model Hub itself is a treasure trove of datasets you can explore and potentially use for fine-tuning.

- **Crowdsourcing:** Online platforms allow you to outsource data labeling tasks to a large pool of workers. This can be a cost-effective way to obtain a large amount of labeled data, but data quality control is crucial.

## Data Cleaning and Preprocessing

Raw data often requires cleaning and preprocessing before it can be used for fine-tuning. This ensures the model receives consistent and high-quality input. Common data cleaning and preprocessing steps include:

- **Handling Missing Values:** Decide how to address missing data points (e.g., remove them, impute them with average values).

- **Normalization:** This might involve converting text to lowercase, removing punctuation, or stemming/lemmatization (reducing words to their root form). The specific normalization techniques depend on your task.

- **Text Cleaning:** Remove special characters, URLs, and HTML tags that might not be relevant for the NLP task.

**Data Splitting for Training and Evaluation**

Once your data is cleaned and preprocessed, you need to split it into distinct sets for training, validation, and testing:

- **Training Set (60-80%):** This is the largest portion of your data used to train the model. The model learns to identify patterns and relationships within the training data.

- **Validation Set (10-20%):** The validation set is used to monitor the model's performance during training. It helps identify potential overfitting and fine-tune hyperparameters (learning rate, optimizer) to improve generalization.

- **Test Set (10-20%):** The unseen test set provides a final evaluation of the fine-tuned model's performance on unseen data. It reflects how well the model generalizes to real-world scenarios beyond the training data.

There are various data splitting strategies, with a common approach being an 80/10/10 split (80% training, 10% validation, 10% test). The ideal split ratio can vary depending on the size and nature of your data.

**Chapter 8: Fine-tuning for Specific NLP Tasks**

Now you're equipped with the knowledge to fine-tune

pre-trained models for real-world NLP tasks! This

chapter showcases how to apply fine-tuning to

various scenarios:

**Fine-tuning for Text Classification**

Imagine you want to build a system that automatically

classifies customer service tickets as high-priority or

low-priority based on their content. Here's a

breakdown of the fine-tuning process for text

classification:

1. **Choose a Pre-trained Model:** Select a model

   from the Hugging Face Hub suitable for text

   classification tasks. Popular options include

   DistilBERT or RoBERTa.

2. **Prepare Your Data:** Collect and label your customer service tickets, categorizing them as high-priority or low-priority. Ensure the data is balanced (roughly equal number of high and low-priority tickets) and representative of real-world scenarios.

## Fine-tune the Model: Unleashing the Classification Powerhouse

We've selected our champion pre-trained model and prepared our data with care. Now, it's time to leverage the power of fine-tuning and transform this pre-trained model into a high-performing classifier for your customer service tickets! Let's delve into the key steps involved:

1. **Load the Pre-trained Model:** Using the Hugging Face Transformers library, you'll load the pre-trained model you selected earlier (e.g., DistilBERT or RoBERTa). The library provides functions to conveniently access models from the Hugging Face Model Hub.

2. **Define the Fine-tuning Task:** Inform the model about the specific task you're aiming to achieve – classifying customer service tickets as high-priority or low-priority. This involves specifying the input format (text) and the output format (two categories – high and low).

3. **Freeze the Base Layers:** Remember, fine-tuning is all about leveraging the pre-trained knowledge while adapting the model to your

specific task. To achieve this, we'll freeze the base layers (initial layers) of the pre-trained model. These layers have already learned valuable linguistic knowledge and don't require significant changes for classifying customer service tickets.

4. **Fine-tune the Final Layers:** The final layers of the pre-trained model are responsible for the specific task output (classification in our case). We'll "unfreeze" these layers and train them on your labeled customer service ticket data. This allows the model to adjust its understanding of language based on the high-priority vs low-priority labels, ultimately enabling it to classify unseen tickets accurately.

5. **Training the Model:** This is where the magic happens! You'll feed your prepared customer service ticket data (text and corresponding labels) to the fine-tuned model. The model will iteratively learn from the data, adjusting the weights and biases in the final layers to improve its classification accuracy.

**Optimizing the Fine-tuning Process:**

While these core steps form the foundation of fine-tuning, there are additional aspects to consider for optimal performance:

- **Choosing an Optimizer:** An optimizer algorithm dictates how the model updates its weights during training. Popular options include Adam or SGD. Experimenting with different optimizers can sometimes lead to better results.

- **Setting the Learning Rate:** The learning rate controls how much the model's weights are updated in each training iteration. A higher learning rate can lead to faster learning but also increase the risk of the model becoming unstable. Techniques like learning rate scheduling can help find the optimal learning rate for your specific task.

- **Batch Size:** The batch size refers to the number of data points processed by the model in each training iteration. A larger batch size can improve training speed but might require more memory. Finding the right batch size for your hardware and dataset is crucial.

**Monitoring and Evaluation:**

It's important to monitor your model's performance during training to avoid overfitting. Overfitting occurs when the model becomes too focused on the specific patterns in your training data and performs poorly on unseen data. Here are some strategies to prevent overfitting:

- **Validation Set:** Set aside a portion of your data (validation set) for monitoring performance during training. This helps you identify when the model starts to overfit and allows you to stop training early if necessary.

- **Early Stopping:** This technique automatically halts training when the model's performance on the validation set starts to decline. This prevents the model from memorizing the training data and ensures it generalizes well to unseen data.

**Evaluation Metrics:**

Once you've fine-tuned your model, it's time to evaluate its performance on unseen data. Here, we'll use metrics like accuracy, precision, recall, and F1-score to assess how well the model classifies your customer service tickets. These metrics provide insights into how well the model identifies high-priority and low-priority tickets accurately.

By following these steps and considering the optimization and evaluation aspects, you'll successfully fine-tune your pre-trained model and equip it with the power to classify your customer service tickets effectively. This fine-tuned model can then be integrated into your customer support system to automate ticket classification, streamline workflows, and improve efficiency.

**Part 4: Advanced Concepts**

Having mastered the fundamentals of fine-tuning, this part delves into advanced concepts to empower you to create robust and efficient NLP applications with Hugging Face Transformers.

## Chapter 9: Pipelines and Text Processing with Transformers

This chapter introduces the concept of pipelines and explores various techniques for processing text data with Transformers.

- **The Power of Pipelines:** Imagine an assembly line for processing text data. Pipelines streamline the NLP workflow by chaining together pre-built processing steps like tokenization (splitting text into units), encoding (converting text into numerical representations), and model inference (applying the fine-tuned model for predictions). The Hugging Face Transformers library provides pre-built pipelines for common NLP tasks, making them easier to implement.

- **Building Custom Pipelines:** While pre-built pipelines offer convenience, you can also construct custom pipelines for specific needs. This chapter will guide you through building a custom pipeline for text classification, allowing you to tailor the processing steps to your exact requirements.

- **Text Preprocessing Techniques:** Beyond tokenization, various preprocessing techniques can enhance the effectiveness of Transformers:
  - **Normalization:** Techniques like converting text to lowercase, removing punctuation, and stemming/lemmatization (reducing words to their root form) can improve model performance.
  - **Stop Word Removal:** Stop words are common words like "the" or "and" that carry little meaning. Removing them can help the model focus on more content-rich words.
  - **Text Augmentation (Optional):** Artificially creating variations of your existing data

(e.g., synonyms, paraphrases) can help the model generalize better and reduce overfitting.

**Chapter 10: Customizing Training and Evaluation**

This chapter empowers you to customize the fine-tuning process by adjusting training configurations and evaluation metrics.

- **Training Configurations:** Fine-tuning involves training the final layers of a pre-trained model on your data. Here, you can customize various training configurations:

- **Learning Rate:** This hyperparameter controls how much the model's weights are updated during training. A higher learning rate can lead to faster learning but also increase the risk of instability. We'll explore strategies for finding the optimal learning rate.

- **Optimizer:** The optimizer algorithm dictates how the model updates its weights based on the errors it makes during training. Popular optimizers include Adam and SGD (Stochastic Gradient

Descent). We'll discuss the advantages and disadvantages of different optimizers.

- **Batch Size:** This refers to the number of data points processed by the model in each training iteration. A larger batch size can improve training speed but might require more memory. We'll explore strategies for choosing an appropriate batch size.

- **Evaluation Metrics:** Beyond accuracy, various metrics help evaluate the performance of your fine-tuned model for specific tasks:

  - **Text Classification:** Metrics like precision, recall, and F1-score measure how well the model identifies the correct categories for your text data.

- Question Answering: Evaluation metrics for question answering might assess how well the retrieved answer passages match the question and their factual correctness.

- Text Summarization: Metrics like ROUGE (Recall-Oriented Understudy for Gisting Evaluation) evaluate the similarity between the generated summaries and human-written summaries.

- Fine-tuning with Early Stopping: To prevent overfitting, a technique called early stopping can be employed. Here, the training process is halted if the model's performance on the validation set starts to decline. This helps ensure

the model generalizes well to unseen data.

## Chapter 11 : Deploying Hugging Face Models in Production

This chapter provides a high-level overview of deploying your fine-tuned Hugging Face models in production environments for real-world use:

- **Understanding Production Deployment:** Once you've fine-tuned a model and achieved satisfactory performance, you might want to deploy it in production. This involves integrating the model into your application or service to process real-world data and generate predictions.

- **Serving Frameworks:** Frameworks like TensorFlow Serving or TorchServe can be used to deploy your fine-tuned model for production use. These frameworks optimize the model for serving requests and ensure efficient inference.

- **Cloud Deployment Considerations:** Cloud platforms offer various options for deploying NLP models. We'll discuss factors to consider when choosing a cloud platform for your NLP application, such as scalability, cost-effectiveness, and ease of use.

- **Security and Monitoring:** When deploying models in production, security considerations are crucial. We'll touch upon best practices for securing your NLP models and monitoring their performance over time.

www.ingramcontent.com/pod-product-compliance
Lightning Source LLC
LaVergne TN
LVHW051700050326
832903LV00032B/3930